LITERATURE ACTIVITIES
FOR
YOUNG CHILDREN

Written by Dianna Sullivan
Illustrated by Nedra L. Pence

Art Projects and Skill Building Activities

for

CHILDREN'S POETRY

selected from

The Real Mother Goose (Checkerboard Press, 1944)

If I Ran the Zoo by Dr. Seuss (Random House, 1950)

Sing a Song of Popcorn selected by Beatrice Schenk de Regniers, et al. (Scholastic Inc., 1988)

Now We Are Six by A. A. Milne (Dell, 1955)

The Random House Book of Poetry for Children selected by Jack Prelutsky
(Random House, 1983)

The Book of Pigericks by Arnold Lobel (Harper & Row, 1983)

Teacher Created Materials
P.O. Box 1214
Huntington Beach, CA 92647
©1991 *Teacher Created Materials, Inc.*
Made in U.S.A.

ISBN 1–55734–299–7

Table of Contents

Note: The page number next to the title indicates the page on which the poem can be found in the original resource.

Extension Ideas

Selecting a Poem

Choose poems that:

1. contain language children will understand
2. reflect children's interests
3. include childhood experiences
4. exhibit a beauty of language
5. are timeless in subject matter

Teaching a Poem

1. Give children background information about the poem.
2. Set the stage for the poem by showing pictures and items that enhance the topic or setting of the poem.
3. Read the poem to the class with enthusiasm, feeling, correct intonations, and clarity.
4. Discuss the poem with the class. Talk about characters, setting, events, descriptive words, moods, content, author's purpose, and unfamiliar words.
5. Reread the poem while the children follow the words silently in their books. The children may whisper the words as the teacher recites the poem.

Extended Teaching Ideas for Poems

1. Children can guess from the title and the picture what the poem is about.
2. Choral Reading:
   - The whole class reads the poem together silently, then aloud.
   - Let girls take the first stanza and the boys the second. Reread the poem, reversing the order.
   - Divide the children into 2, 3, or 4 groups. Each group reads one stanza in unison.
   - One child reads a line or more solo; the class reads the stanza.
   - Choose several good readers to read a stanza aloud.

3. Children can explore the pictures surrounding a poem, then relate their own experiences (things they see, hear, taste, smell, touch).
4. Have children read aloud parts of a poem. For example, have them choose:
   - the funniest parts
   - descriptive words for a character, place, or thing
   - mood words

5. Draw pictures illustrating the incidents or stanzas of a poem.
6. Copy words, lines, stanzas, or the whole poem from the board onto paper.

Extension Ideas *(cont.)*

7. Have children make a display of physical objects mentioned in a poem.

8. Class may interpret the actions of a poem in pantomime. Dramatize parts or the whole poem or act out poems with finger plays.

9. Children may memorize a poem and recite the poem to the teacher, in front of a small group, or in front of the class. Offer stickers or small trinkets as rewards for poem memorization!

10. Encourage children to learn about the authors/illustrators of poems. Write a group story about the author or illustrator.

11. Recite or list rhyming words in the poem for fun skill-building.

12. Have the children think of questions they would like to ask the main character. Questions can be asked verbally, listed on paper, or listed on the board.

13. Collect poems. Have children draw pictures depicting the poems. Bind child-illustrated poems into a classroom book. Place the book in the library corner for everyone to enjoy.

14. Make a mural of the poem depicting the characters, scenes, and mood(s) of the poem.

15. Copy a poem and glue it onto construction paper. Have the children illustrate the poem. Hang the poster on a wall for all to enjoy.

16. Have the children invent their own word pictures (similes). For example, suggest ''as quick as bunnies,''''as red as apples,''or ''as scary as _____.''

17. Children write their own free verse poems in a ready-made framework. For example, use:

    I wish I could _____ .
    I wish I were _____ .
    Happiness is _____ .

18. Read and write poems depicting the seasons or holidays. Collect them into your own holiday or season booklet.

19. Compare one poem with another.

20. With the help of the music teacher, have the children invent music for poems (or, poems for music!).

Little Boy Blue

1. Color and cut out boy on pages 5 and 6.

2. Punch out holes A-D.

3. Attach boy's arms and legs to his body by inserting paper fasteners through holes A-D matching like letters.

diagram

Little Boy Blue

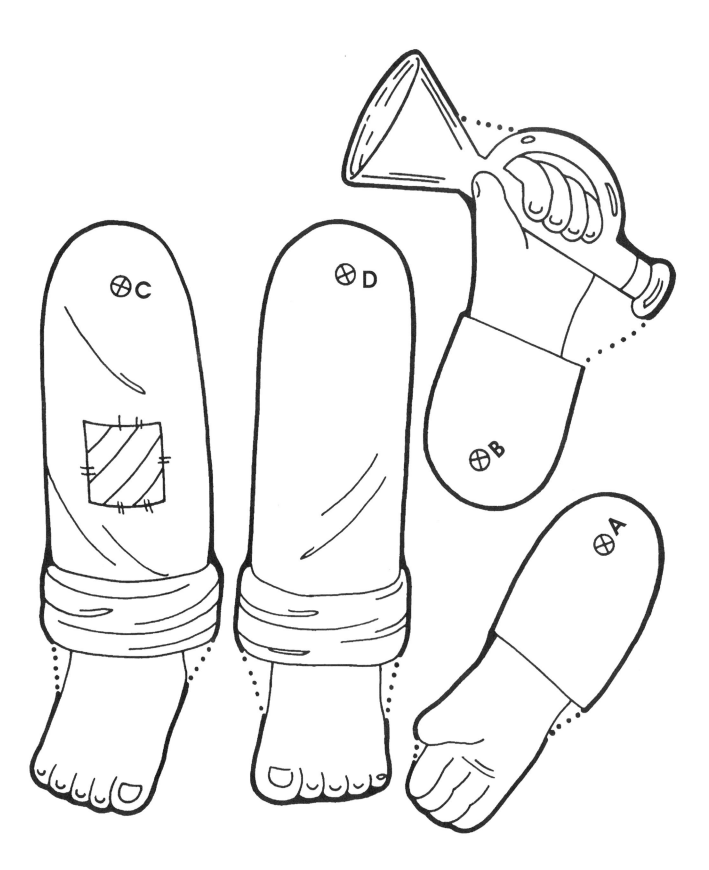

Little Bo-Peep

1. Color and cut out girl on pages 7 and 8.

2. Attach bottom of girl to the top, tab A, page 7.

diagram

Tab C

Tab A

Little Bo-Peep

3. **Arms:** Attach arms to girl's body behind her shoulders at tabs B and C.

4. **Sheep:** Glue the girl's hands onto the sheep.

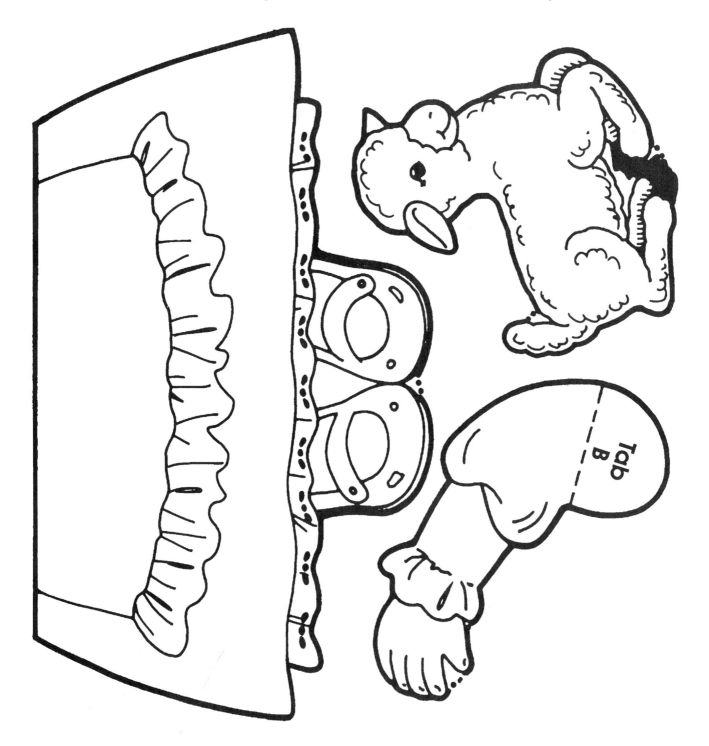

Name_____

Hush-a-Bye

 and the poem to the correct pictures.

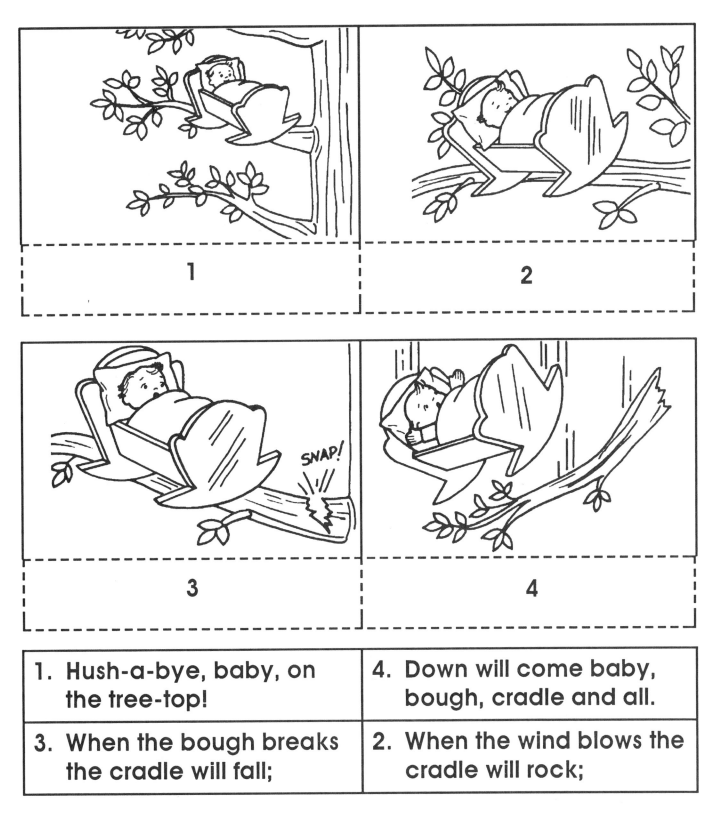

1. Hush-a-bye, baby, on the tree-top!	4. Down will come baby, bough, cradle and all.
3. When the bough breaks the cradle will fall;	2. When the wind blows the cradle will rock;

Pussy-Cat and Queen

the path from the cat to the queen.

Name_____   *The Real Mother Goose*

Wee Willie Winkie

, ✂ , the pictures that are alike side by side.

11   *#299 Literature Activities for Young Children*

Little Miss Muffet

1. Color and cut out spider on pages 12 and 13. Cut slits A-D on spider's body.

2. Legs: Fold tabs A-D under. Push the leg pieces into the slits on spider's body. Flatten out tabs A-D.

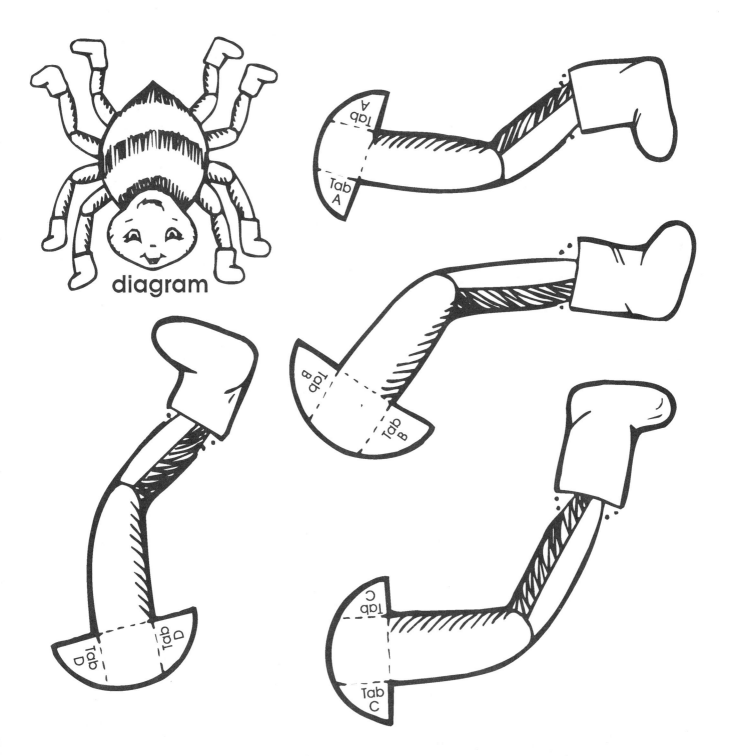

diagram

Little Miss Muffet (cont.)

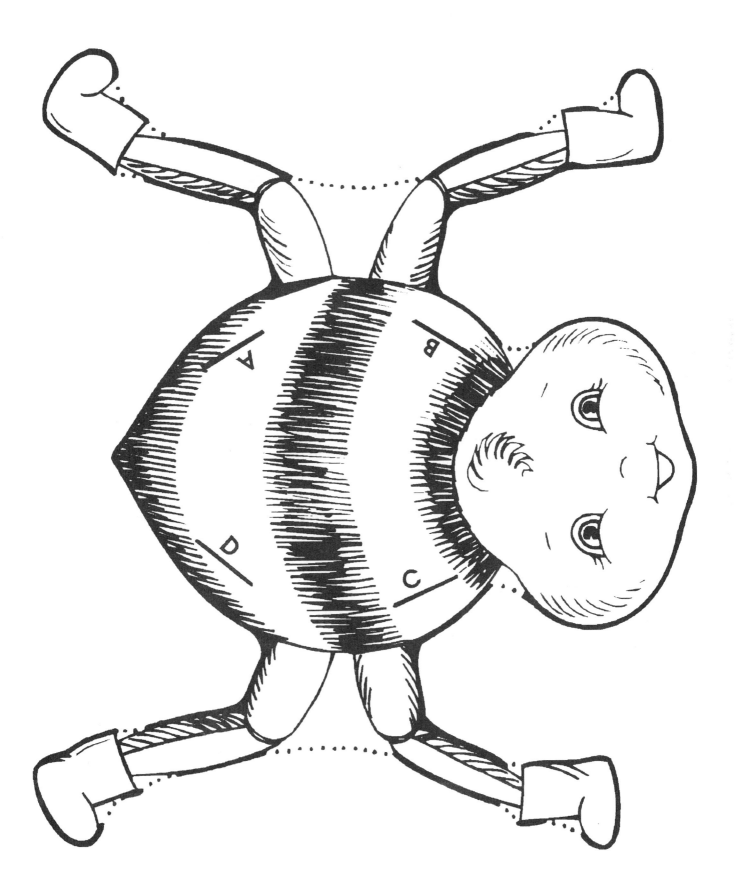

Humpty Dumpty

1. Color and cut out the Humpty Dumpty on this page.

2. Punch out holes A-D.

3. Attach the head to the body with string. Match like letters.

4. Attach the body to the legs with string. Match like letters.

diagram

Old Mother Hubbard

1. Color and cut out the dog pieces pages 15 and 16.

2. Glue the bottom half of dog onto the top half of dog, Tab A, page 15.

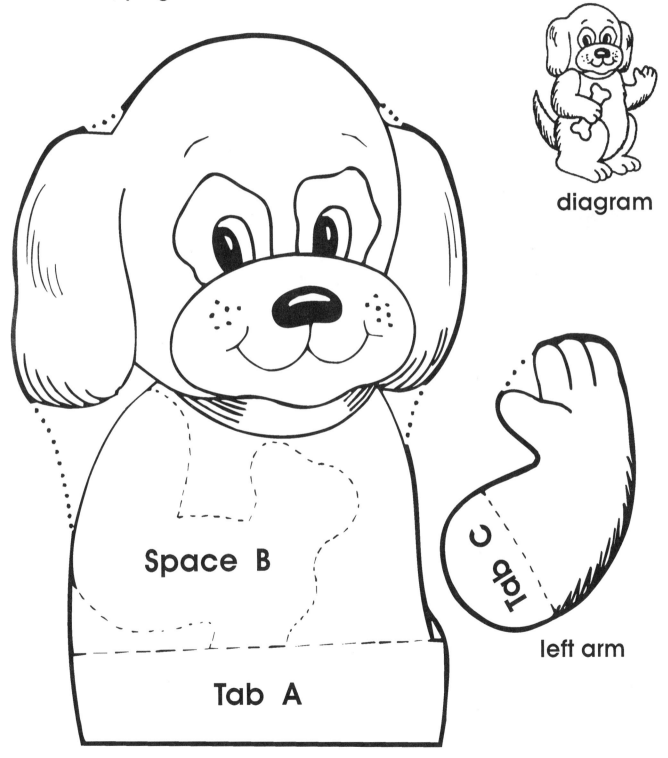

diagram

Space B

Tab C

left arm

Tab A

Old Mother Hubbard *(cont.)*

3. Glue dog's right arm on top of dog's body, space B.

4. Glue dog's left arm behind dog's body on Tab C.

5. Glue dog's tail behind dog's body on Tab D.

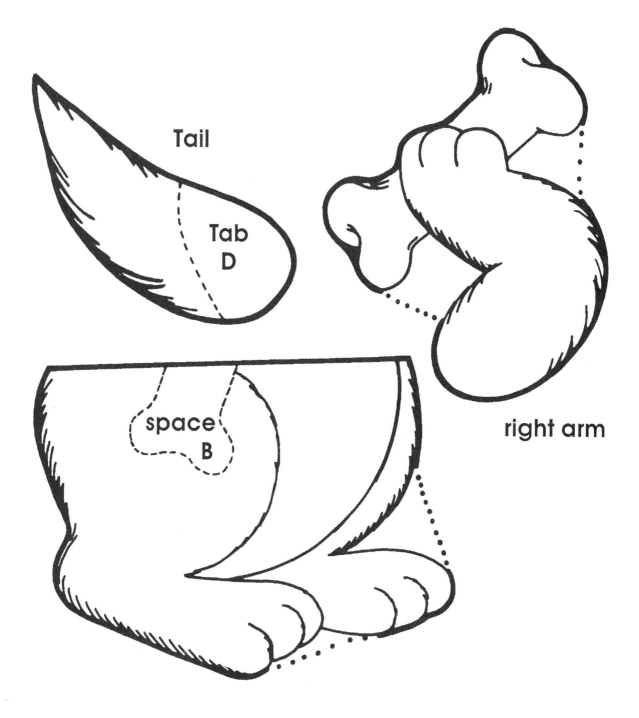

Tail

Tab D

right arm

space B

The Cat and the Fiddle

Copy the cat puzzle on this page five times. Copy the circles on page 18. Color and cut them out. Glue the large picture on the front half of the cat. Glue the same but smaller picture, on the back half of the cat. Cut out and laminate pieces. Children complete cat puzzles by matching the large picture to the same smaller picture.

The Cat and the Fiddle *(cont.)*

Mary, Mary, Quite Contrary

1. Color and cut out the project pieces on pages 19 - 21.

2. Glue the girl's top half to her bottom half, Tab A, page 20.

3. Cut out the space on the girl's top half.

diagram

B

cut out

Mary, Mary, Quite Contrary *(cont.)*

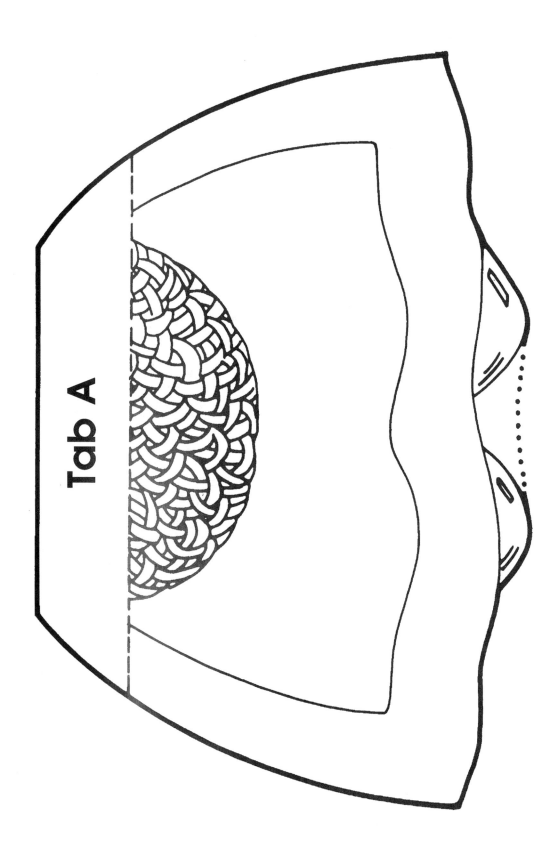

Tab A

Mary, Mary, Quite Contrary *(cont.)*

4. Punch out holes B.

5. Fasten the wheel behind the girl with a paper fastener through holes B. The flowers will show through the basket.

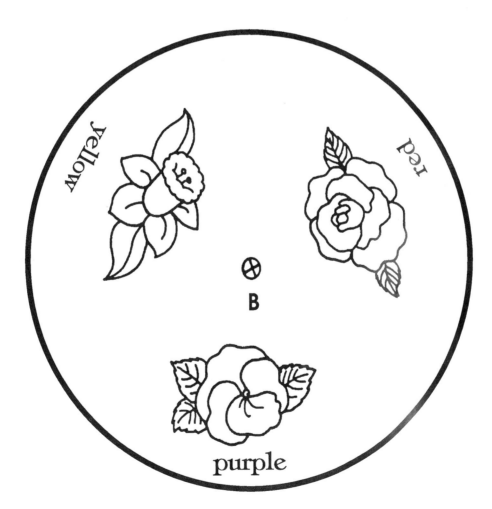

Name_____

Mary, Mary, Quite Contrary

Flowers in the Garden

Copy the garden once (page 22), flowers, and number cards three times (page 23). Color, cut out, laminate. Lay the flower pieces in the garden. Shuffle the number cards. Place face down in a pile. Child draws top card, reads the number. He/she takes ("picks"), that many flowers from the garden. If flowers remain in the garden, the child takes another card until no flowers are left.

diagram

Mary, Mary, Quite Contrary

Flowers in the Garden *(cont.)*

Little Jack Horner

 the big plums purple.

 the little plums red.

There Was an Old Woman

1. Color and cut out shoe and flaps on this page.

2. Attach Flaps A-C on top of Tabs A-C.

diagram

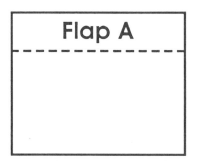

Flap A

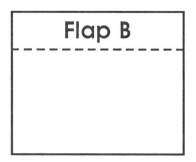

Flap B

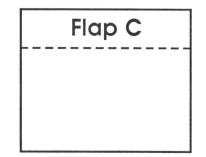

Flap C

The Old Woman Who Lived in a Shoe

Copy the shoe on this page, and number cards on page 27. Color, cut out, laminate. Put a pile of plastic babies (found in craft and dime stores) beside the shoe. Shuffle the number cards and place them face down in a pile. Child draws top card and reads the number. After counting that many babies, the child places them on the shoe. Child removes the babies from the shoe and takes a new top card, repeating the process.

diagram

The Old Woman Who Lived in a Shoe *(cont.)*

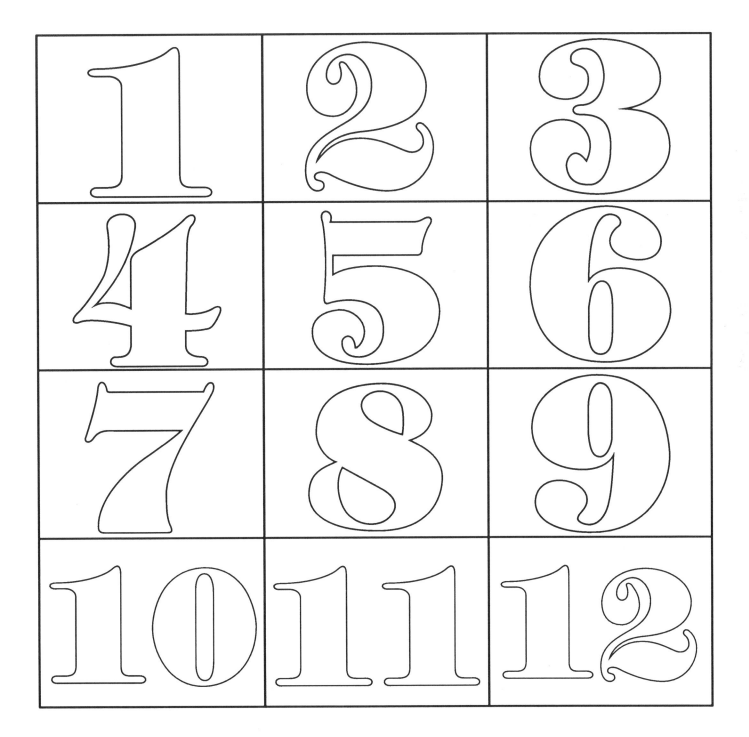

Hickory, Dickory, Dock!

Copy the clock and mouse on this page ten times. On each clock's bird and each mouse, draw and fill in one of the following shapes: circles, squares, triangles, rectangles, ovals, hearts, half moons, eggs, stars, or diamonds. Color, cut out, laminate pieces. Child matches shape on mouse to like shape on clock.

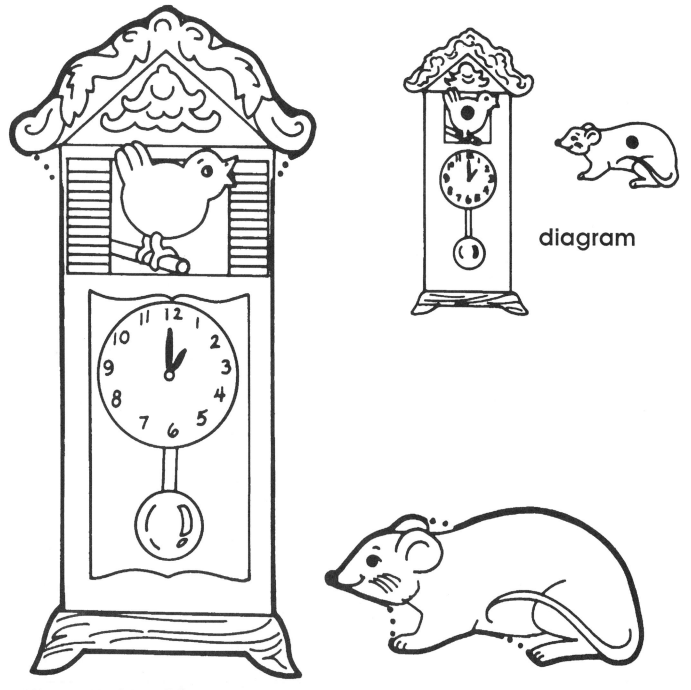

diagram

If I Ran the Zoo

1. Color and cut out the animal on pages 29 and 30. Cut slits on animal's body.

2. Glue animal's back end (page 30) to tab A.

3. Ear: Fold tabs B and C under. Push the ear piece into the straight line on animal's head. Flatten out Tabs B and C.

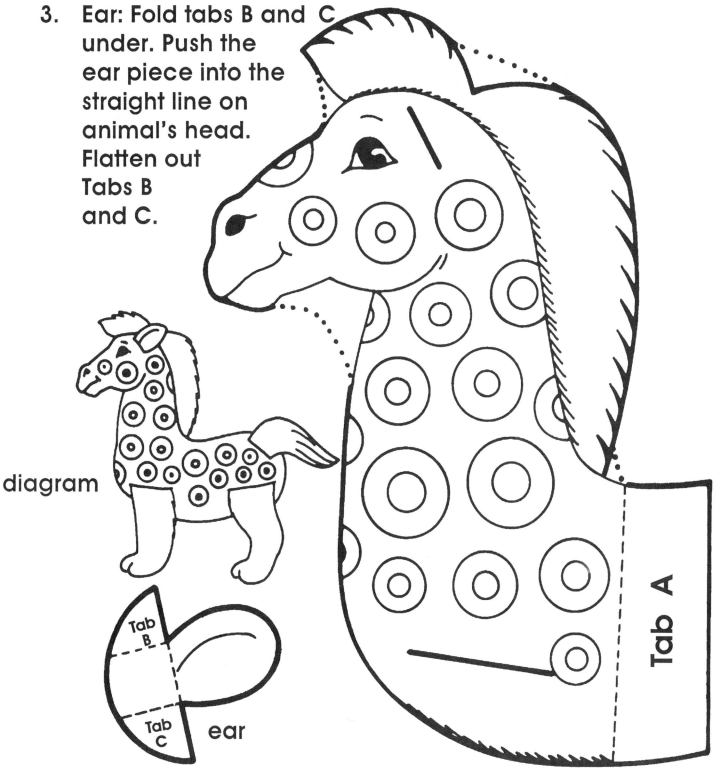

diagram

Tab A

Tab B

Tab C

ear

If I Ran the Zoo *(cont.)*

4. **Tail and Legs:** Fold Tabs D-I under. Push the tail and feet pieces into the slits on animal's body. Flatten out Tabs D-I.

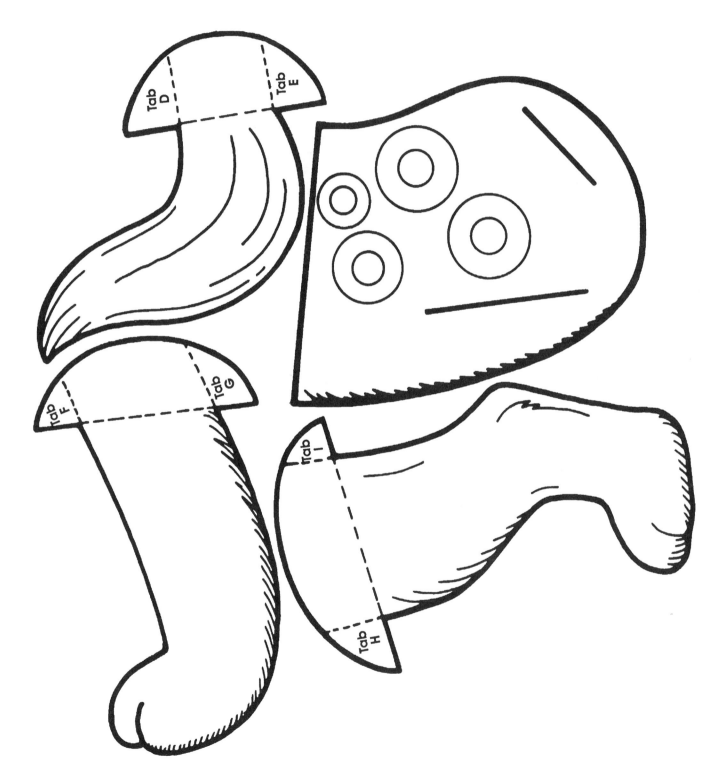

Lion with Ten Feet

1. Color and cut out lion on pages 31 and 32.

2. Glue front half of lion to Tab A, page 32.

3. Punch out holes B-F.

4. Attach lion's feet to lion's body by inserting paper fasteners through holes B-F. Be sure to match like letters.

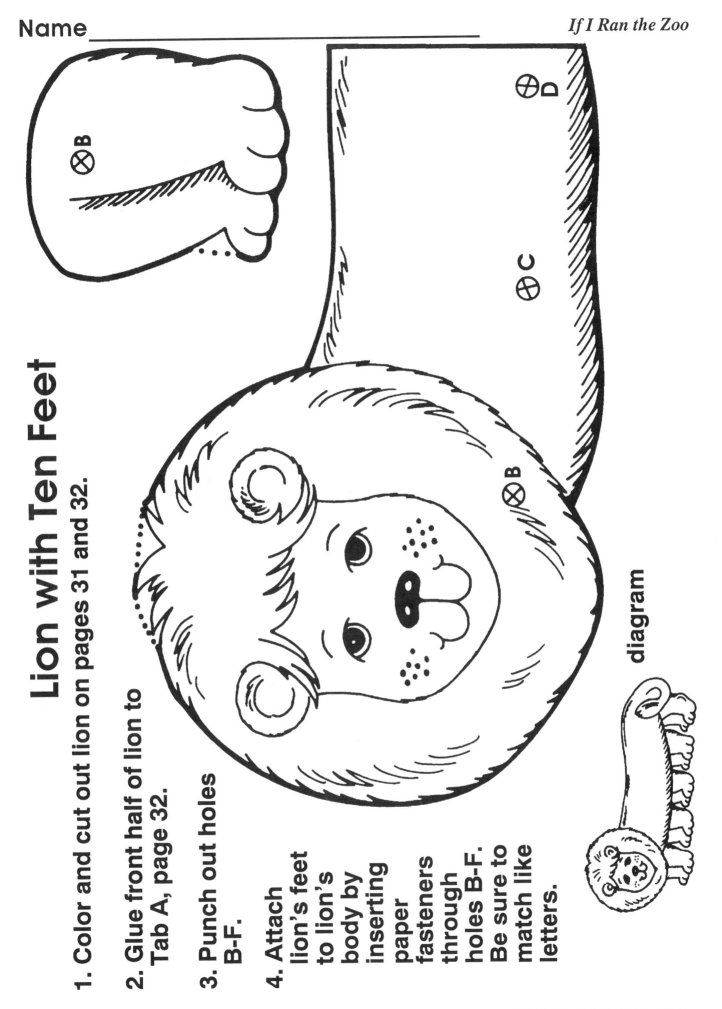

diagram

31 *#299 Literature Activities for Young Children*

Lion with Ten Feet *(cont.)*

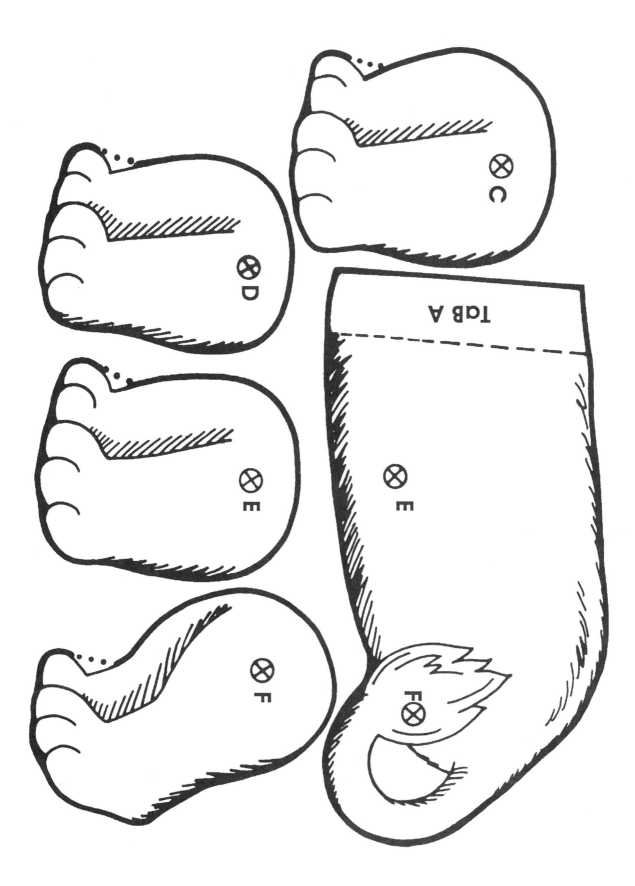

A Sort-of-a-Hen

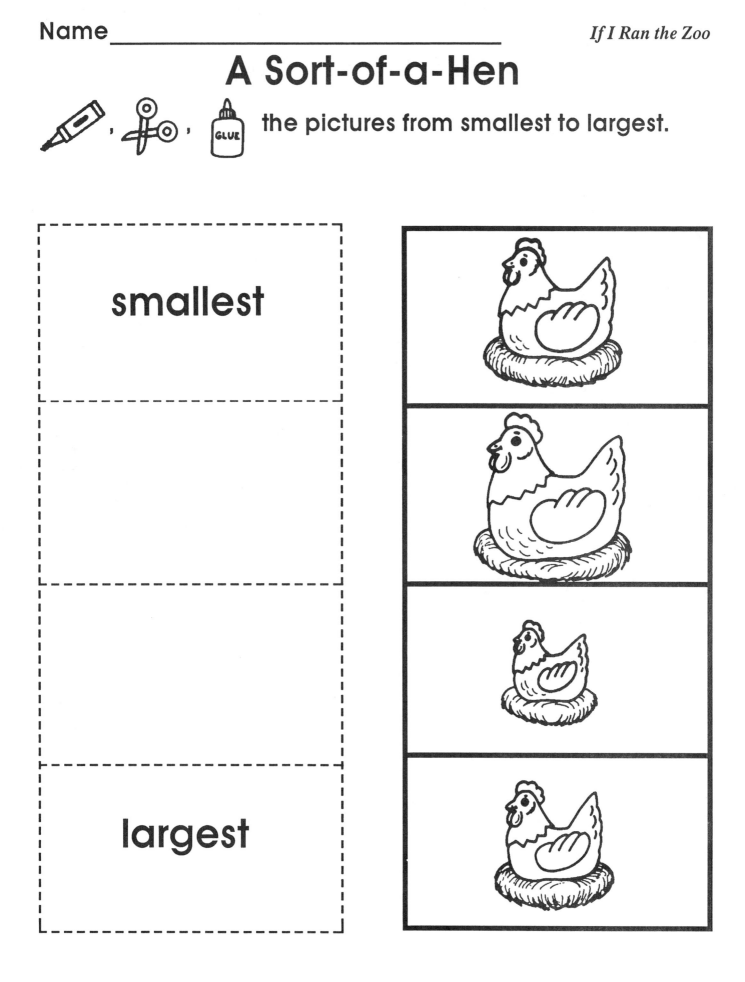

, , GLUE the pictures from smallest to largest.

smallest

largest

The Elephant-Cat

1. Color and cut out the elephant-cat pieces pages 34 and 35.

2. Glue the back half of the elephant-cat to the front half, Tab A, page 35.

diagram

The Elephant-Cat (cont.)

Tab A

Joat

1. Color and cut out Joat pieces on pages 36 and 37.

2. Glue the bottom half of the Joat to Tab A, page 36.

3. Apply glue along Tab B of Joat.

diagram

Tab A

Name ___________________________________

Joat *(cont.)*

4. Lay the pocket on top of Tab B.
5. Color and cut out the card pieces on page 38.
6. Match the opposite Joats.
7. Put the cards into the pocket.

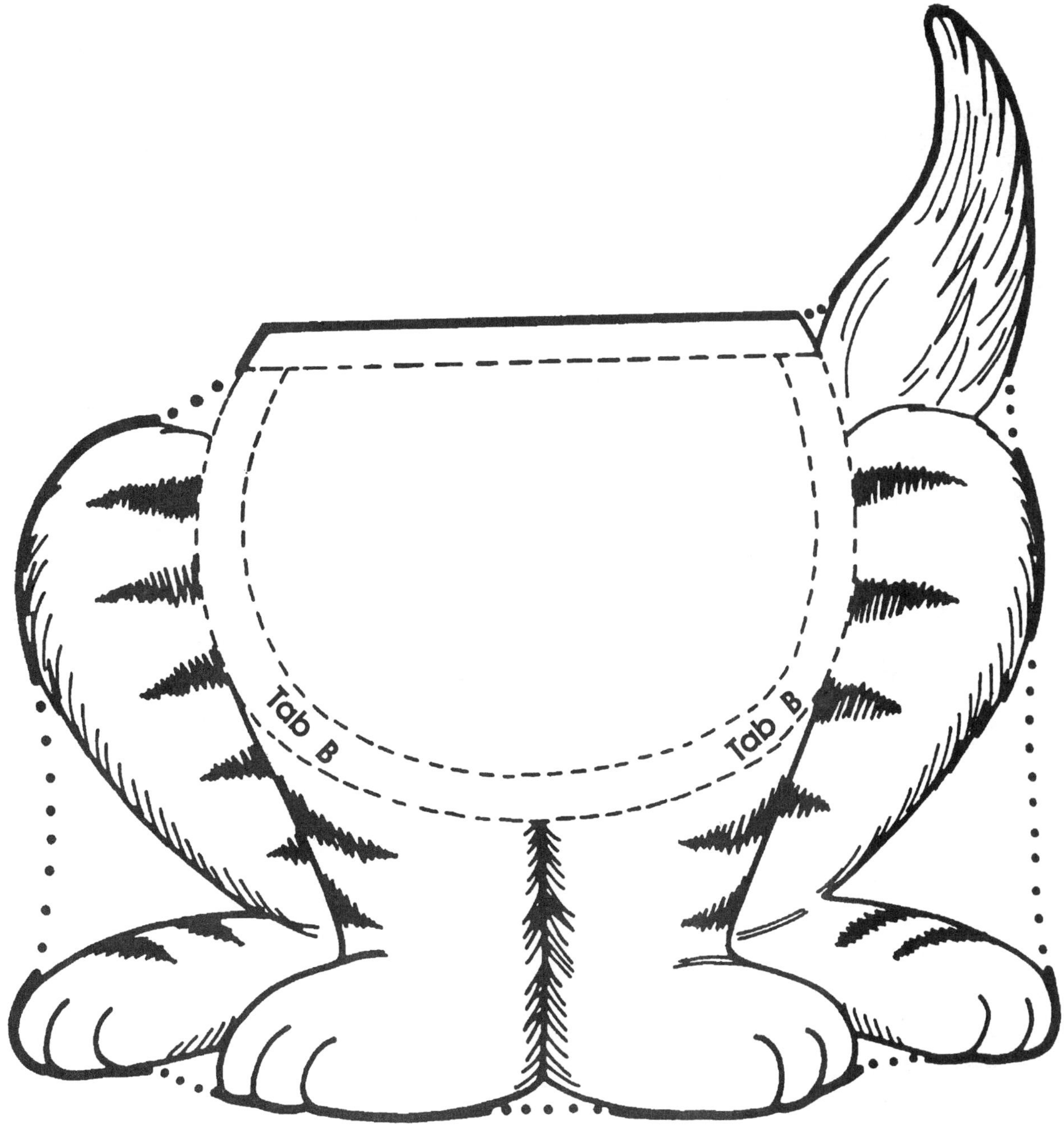

Joat *(cont.)*

hot

cold

up

down

fat

thin

tall

short

A Horned Deer

the path from the deer to the zoo.

A Thwerll

1. Color and cut out the Thwerll project pieces on pages 40 and 41.

2. Glue the pieces to a paper lunch bag.

diagram

A Thwerll *(cont.)*

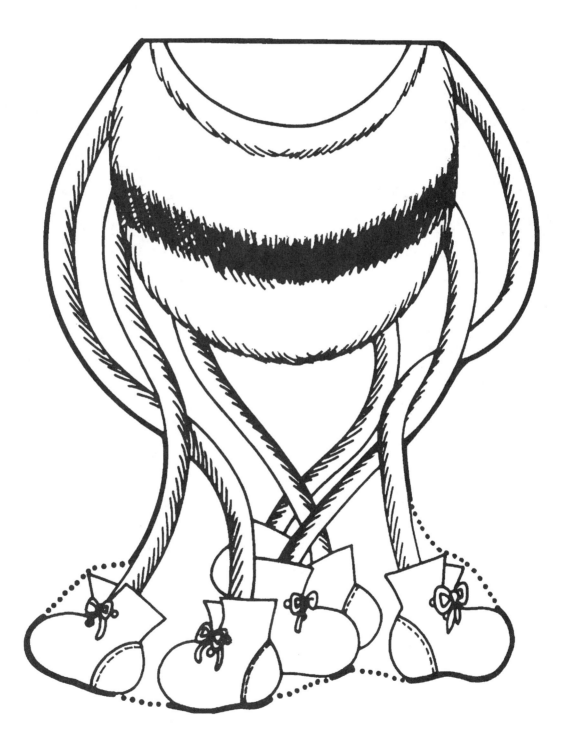

Chuggs the Bean-Shooter Bugs

 the objects.

a line matching like color bugs.

red

yellow

green

red

yellow

green

Zoo Creature Puzzle Game

Copy the creature puzzle on page 43 five times. Copy the rectangles on page 44 once. Cut out the rectangles. Glue the mother animal picture on the back half of the creature. Glue the baby animal picture on the front half of the creature. Cut out, laminate pieces. Child completes creature puzzles by matching the mother half to her correct baby half.

diagram

Zoo Creature Puzzle Game

Five Little Squirrels

1. Color and cut out squirrels. Attach stick to back.

2. Use the puppets to act out the poem.

Name_____

Our Tree

 , ✂ , 🧴 the pictures in order.

1	**2**
spring	summer
3	**4**
autumn	winter

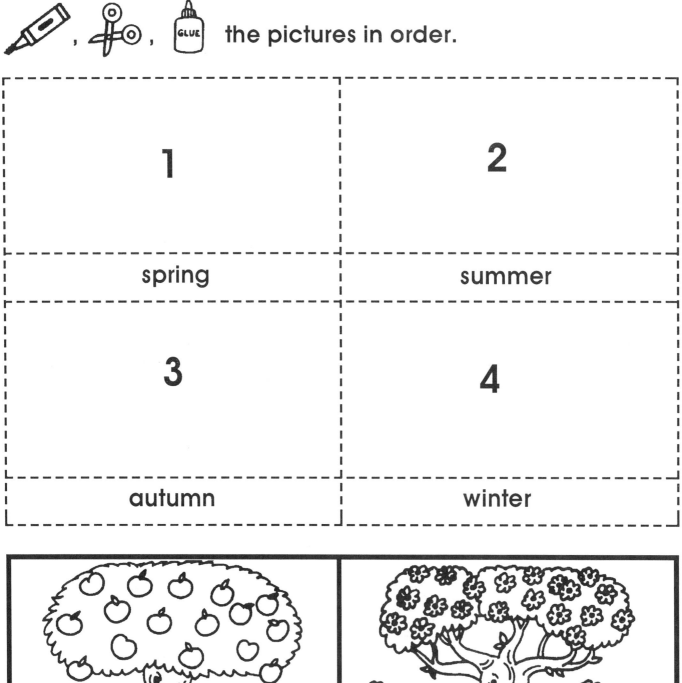

The Bat

1. Color and cut out the bat pieces on this page.

2. Glue the bat body onto the bat wing, Tab A.

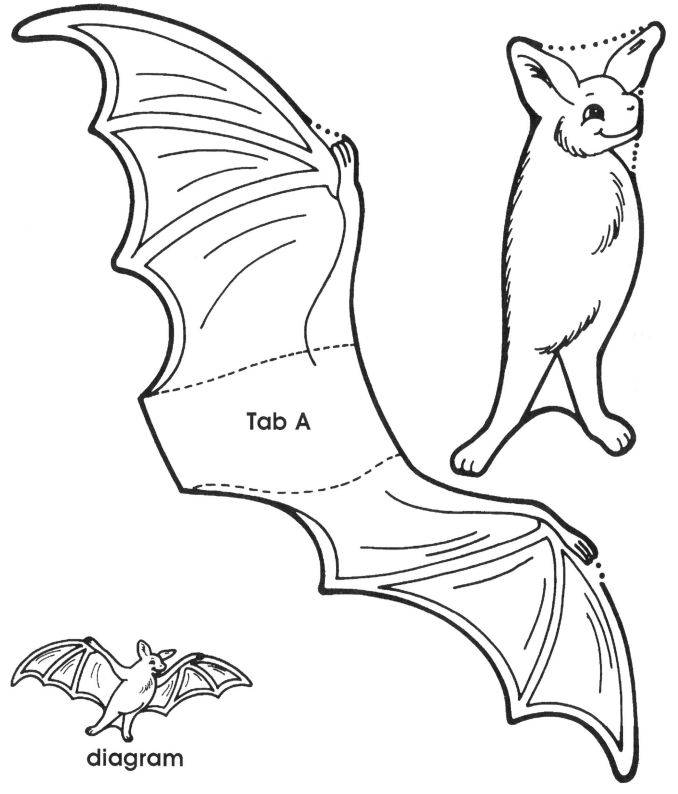

Tab A

diagram

There Was a Crooked Man

1. Color and cut out man pieces on pages 48 and 49.

2. Glue top half of man to his lower body, Tab A, page 49.

3. Apply glue along Tab B of man.

4. Lay the pocket on top of tab B.

There Was a Crooked Man *(cont.)*

diagram

pocket

5. Color and cut out the card pieces on page 50.

6. Retell the rhyme in order, using the cards.

7. Put the cards into the pocket.

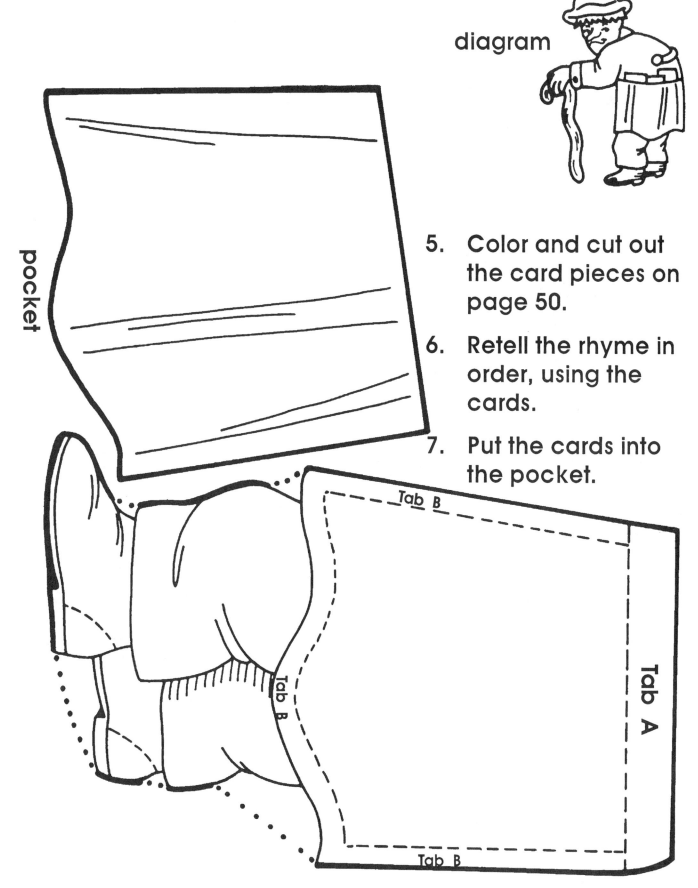

Tab B

Tab B

Tab A

Tab B

There Was a Crooked Man *(cont.)*

Dogs

1. Color and cut out the dog art project pieces on pages 51 and 52.

2. Glue the pieces to a paper lunch bag.

diagram

Dogs (cont.)

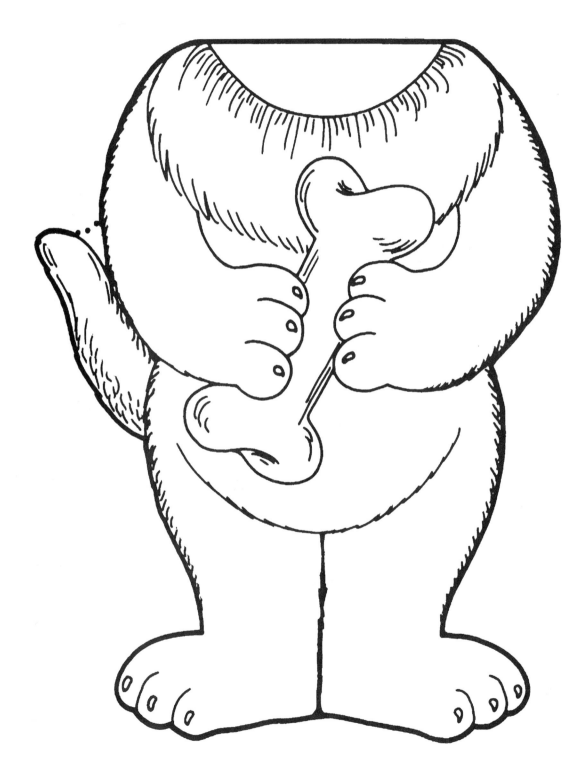

Name_____

Little Snail

Follow the dots from 1-26.

 the snail.

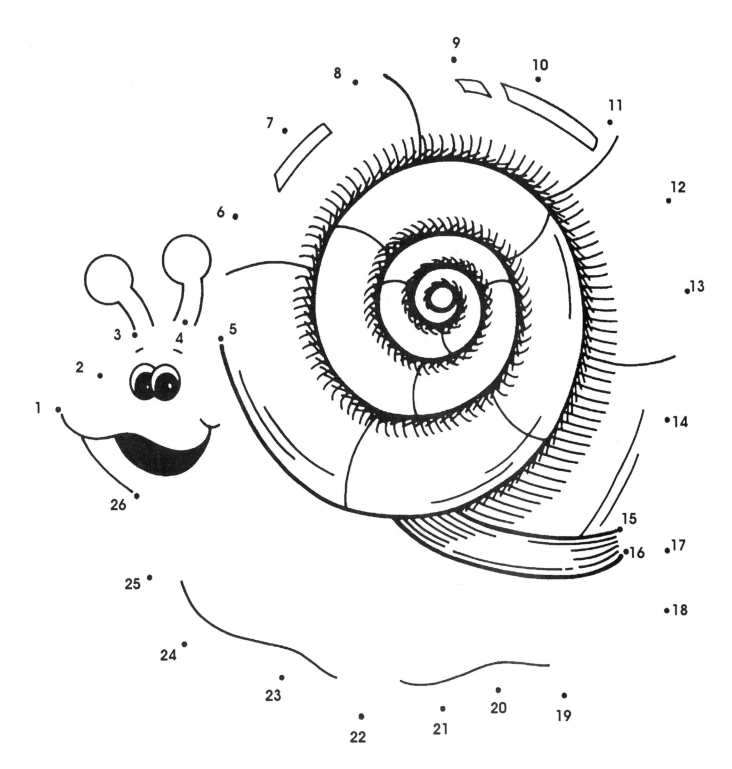

Brother

1. Reproduce the pieces on this page 26 times.

2. Color and cut out.

3. Print capital letters on the big brother. Print lower case letters on the little brother.

4. Children match the upper case letters to the lower case letters.

diagram

What Is Pink?

the color word.   the pictures.

King John's Christmas

Copy the King's halves on this page five times. Color and cut out. Print a numeral on the top half of the King. Draw sets of dots on the King's bottom half that correspond to the number on the King's top half. Laminate. Child matches the number on the King's top half to the correct set of dots on the King's bottom half.

diagram

Sneezles

1. Color and cut out boy pieces pages 57 and 58.

2. Attach the top half of the boy to his bottom half, Tab A, page 58.

3. Arms: Attach Tabs B and C to boy's body behind his shoulders.

Tab B

diagram

Sneezles *(cont.)*

Tab A

Tab C

4. **Bear:** Glue the boy's hands onto the bear.

Us Two

1. Color and cut out bear pieces on pages 59 and 60.

2. Glue bottom half of the bear to Tab A, page 59.

Tab A

diagram

Us Two *(cont.)*

3. Apply glue along Tab B of bear.

4. Lay the pocket on top of Tab B.

5. Color and cut out the card pieces on page 61.

6. Print a number word (one to six) on back of each card. Child sequences number words.

7. Put the cards into the pocket.

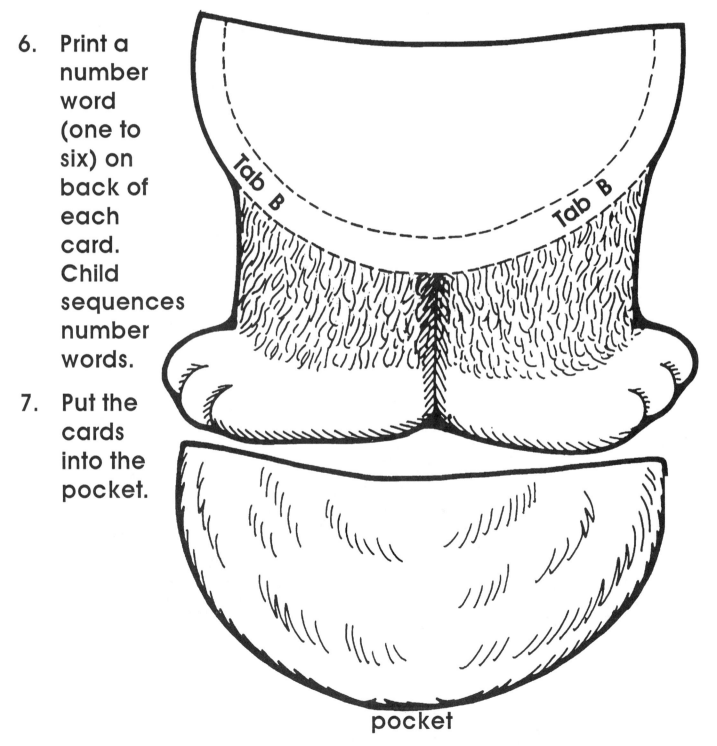

pocket

Name_____

Us Two *(cont.)*

The Engineer

1. Color and cut train art project pieces pages 62 and 63.

2. Punch out holes A-C.

3. Attach the cars together with string. Be sure to attach like letters from car to car, so the cars will be in the correct order.

diagram

The Engineer

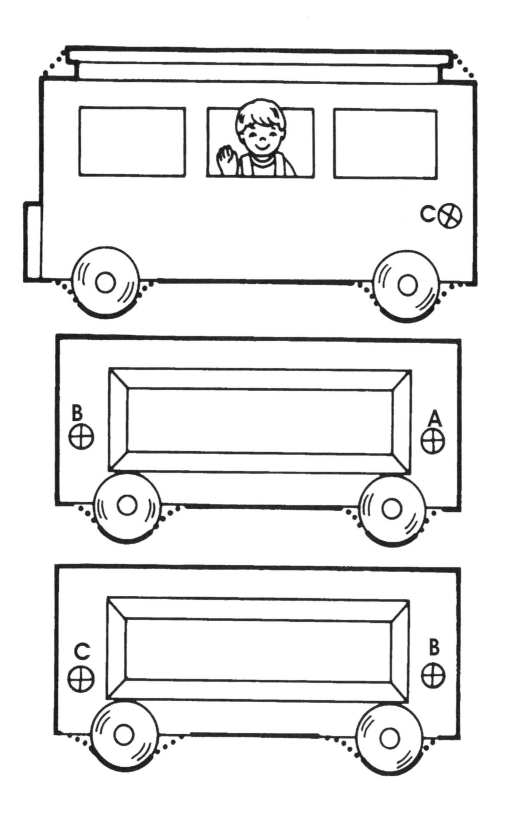

Furry Bear

Reproduce the bear cards on this page, 26 times. Print capital letters on mother bear cards. Print lower case letters on baby bear cards. Color, cut out, and laminate. Children can sequence all capital letters, sequence all lower case letters, or match capital to lower case letters.

diagram

Down by the Pond

 , , GLUE the pictures that are alike.

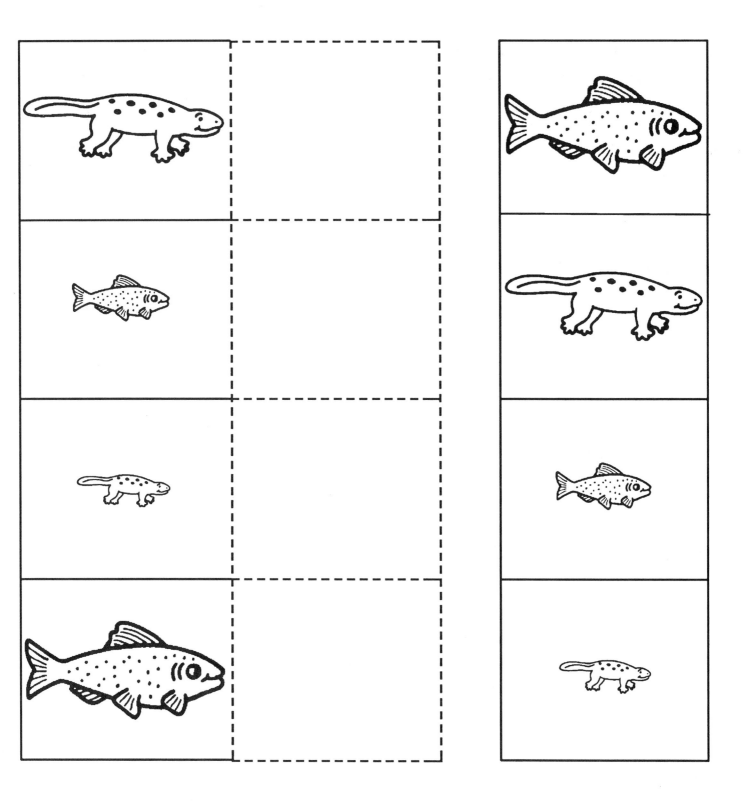

Name_____

The Little Black Hen

1. Reproduce, color, and cut out the pieces on this page ten times.

2. Print a number 1-10 on each of the hens.

3. Read the number on the hen. Child counts out correct number of eggs to correspond to number on hen.

diagram

The Good Little Girl

 the picture.

Name_____

Dogs and Cats and Bears and Bats

the pictures that are the other half of the mammals.

Name_____

Nature Is

Help the bee find the flower.

The Four Seasons

the pictures into the correct group.

summer	fall
winter	spring

The Ways of Living Things

the pictures.

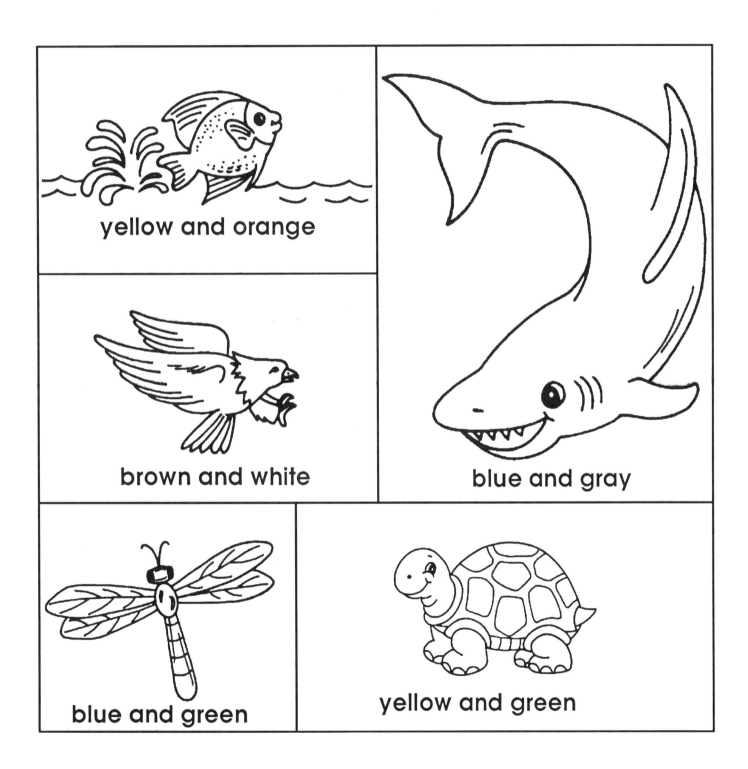

yellow and orange

brown and white

blue and gray

blue and green

yellow and green

Children, Children Everywhere

1. Color and cut out the children on pages 72 and 73.

2. Glue children together so they are holding hands.

Children, Children, Everywhere (cont.)

Poor Old Lady

1. Color and cut out lady art pieces pages 74 and 75.

2. Attach top half of lady to bottom half of lady, Tab A, page 75.

cut out

diagram

Poor Old Lady *(cont.)*

3. Cut out space on lady's face and slit in lady's hair.

4. Glue tab piece to a 2 1/2" x 11" (6.25 cm x 27.5 cm) strip of heavy paper so that about 2" (5 cm) of the paper extends at each end.

5. Push the tab piece through the slit, behind the lady's head. The things the lady eats will show in her mouth.

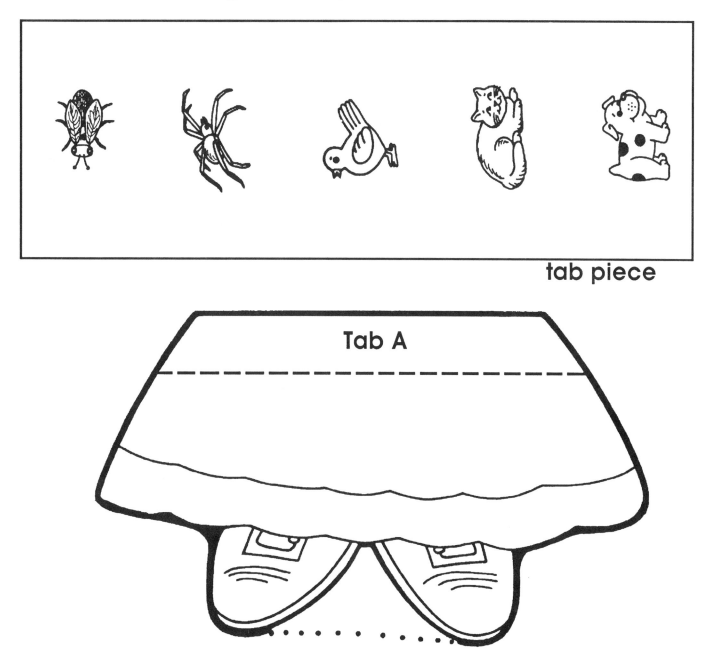

tab piece

Tab A

Nonsense!

 the things that happen in the poem.

The Seven Ages of Elf-Hood

1. Color and cut out the elf on pages 77 and 78. Cut slits on elf's body.

2. Glue top half of elf to bottom half of elf, Tab A, page 78.

The Seven Ages of Elf-Hood*(cont.)*

Arms: Fold Tabs B-E under. Push the arm pieces into the slits on elf's chest. Flatten out tabs B-E.

diagram

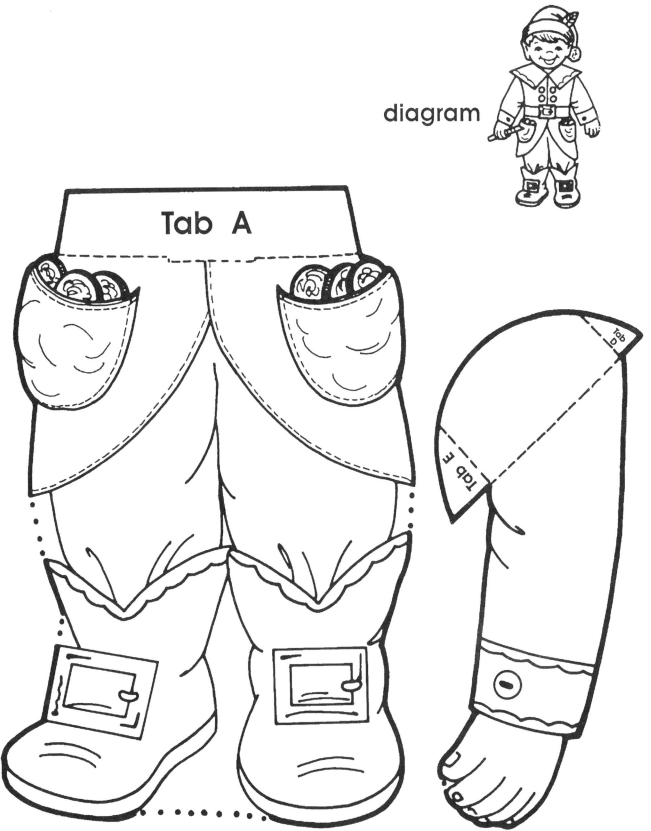

Tab A

Tab D

Tab E

The Land of Potpourri

1. Reproduce, color, and cut out the pieces on this page 26 times.

2. Print capital letters on the engines. Print lower case letters on the caboose.

3. Have children match the upper case letters to the lower case letters.

diagram

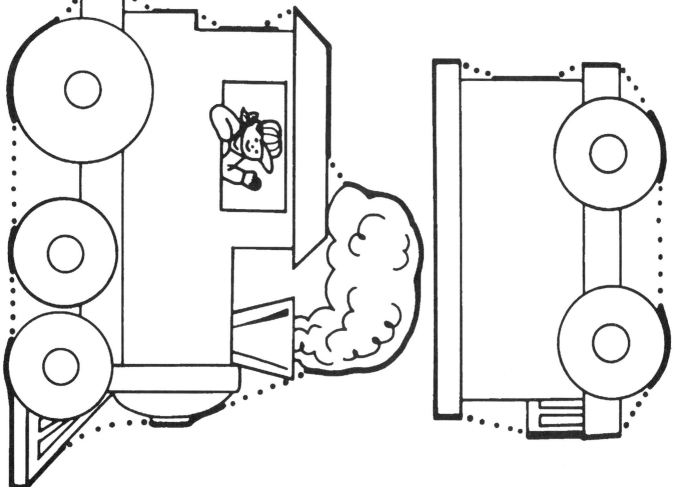

Name_____

Writing a Story or Verse

Help the pig  a story or verse. Draw a picture about your story.

Moths on the Ceiling

, , six moths on the ceiling.

The Curly-Tailed Pig

1. Color and cut out circle pieces.

2. Tape a craft stick to each piece for a hand puppet.

3. Have the child retell story with the pieces.

Name_____

Escaping from a Whale!

Help the pig get to a safe place.

Name_____

Washed Away Sandcastle

, , **GLUE** the pictures in order.

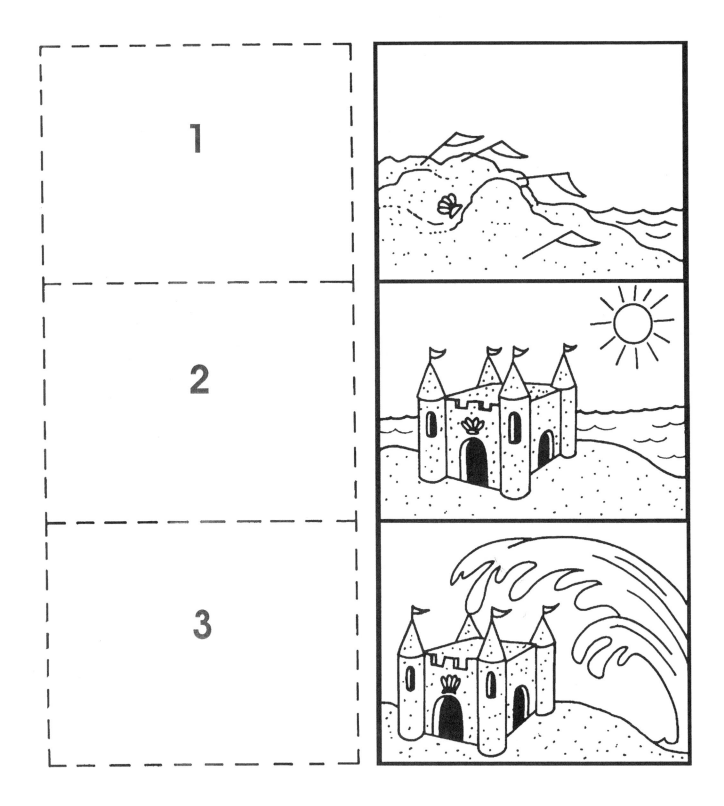

Name_____

A Cold Pig

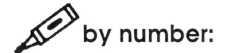 by number:

1- red 2-yellow 3-orange 4-green 5-blue

The Rich Pig

 ,  ,  the pieces onto a piece of construction paper. Make a pig picture.

The Musical Pig

 ,  the pieces where they belong.

The Pig's Clock

Clock Numerals - Game #1

Copy the clock. Color, cut out, laminate. Provide the child with a set of plastic numerals. Child places the numerals in the correct position on the clock.

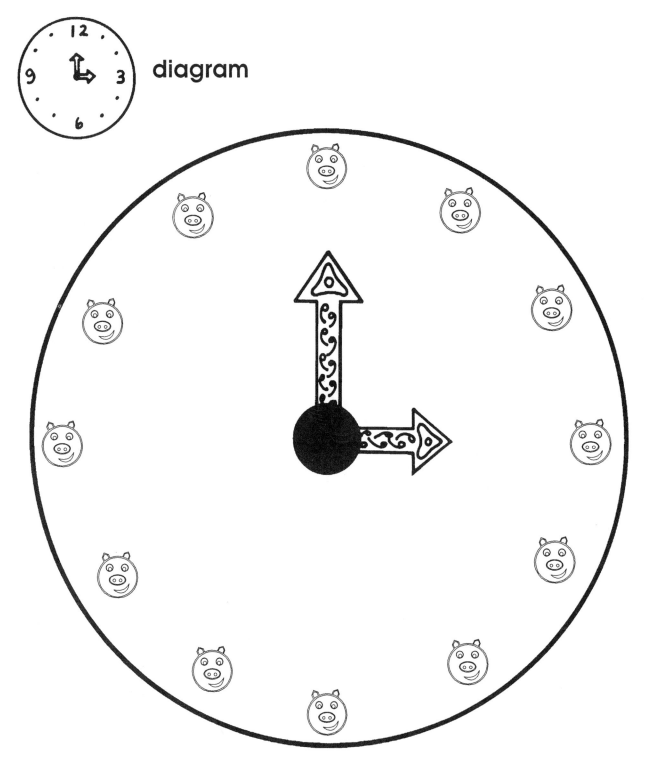

diagram

The Pig's Clock

Complete the Clock Face - Game #2

Copy the clock and numeral cards pages 88 and 89.
Color, cut out, and laminate. Shuffle the twelve cards face
down. Divide up the twelve cards between two players.
Each player turns his/her cards face up. Roll two dice;
both children count the dots that are showing. The child
with the numeral card that matches the number of dots
puts his/her card on the clock in the correct place. The
above process is continued until one of the children has
ALL his cards on the clock.

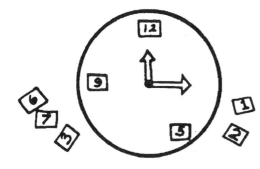

diagram

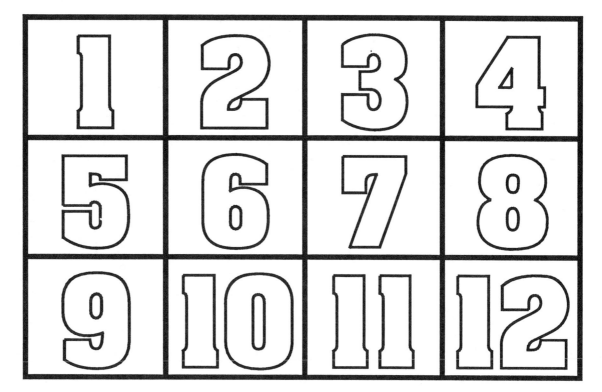

The Flatten Pig

1. ✏️ a line connecting the number to a picture. Put the pictures in 1-2-3 order from fat to flat.

2. Color the pictures.

The Pig's Breakfast

, , the pictures where they belong.

first	second

second   first

Name_____

Pig Caught in the Rain

 ,  ,  the pictures that are alike.

The Bird Pig

the pictures where they belong.

The Stiff Pig

Name_____

, , the pieces in order onto construction paper. Make a picture.

diagram

Name_____

Frogs and Toads in a Pocket

1. Color and cut out pig on pages 95 and 96.

2. Glue top half of pig to Tab A, page 95.

3. Punch out holes B-C.

4. Attach pig's arms to pig's body by inserting paper fasteners through holes B-C matching like letters.

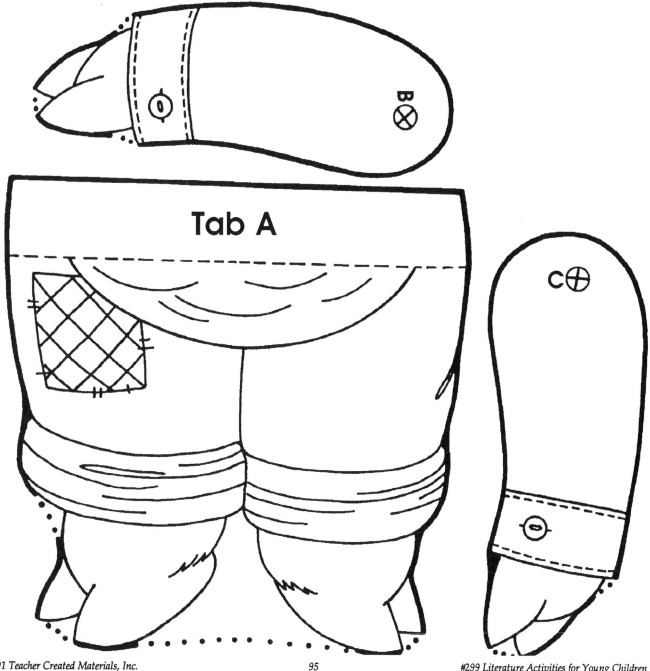

Frogs and Toads in a Pocket *(cont.)*

diagram